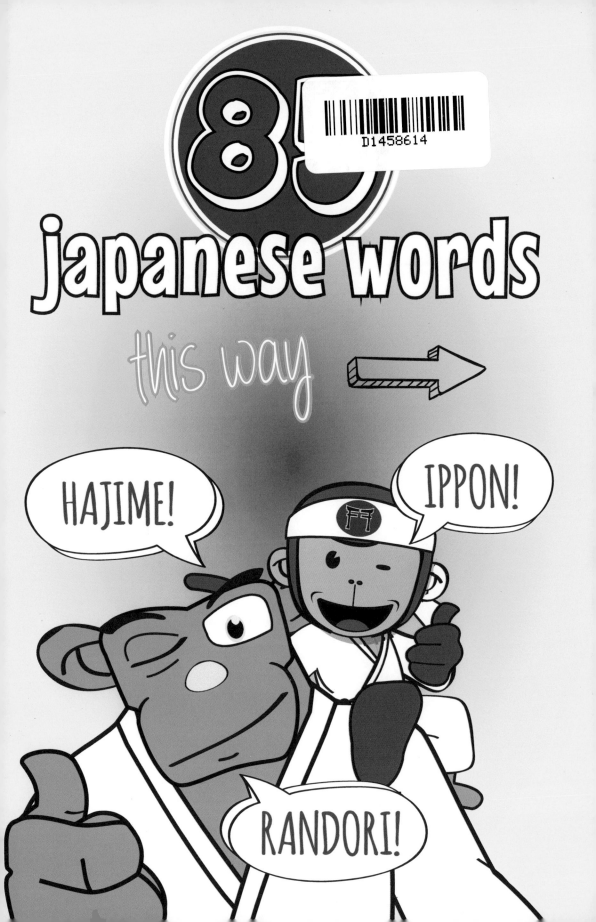

First published by Koka Kids, 2020
Copyright © Nicola Fairbrother, 2020
Illustrations by Jose Obrador
www.kokakids.co.uk

A MESSAGE FROM OLYMPIC SILVER MEDALLIST
NiK FAiRBROTHER

> HAJIME!

You are about to learn 85 Japanese judo words!

Learning Japanese terminology is a part of learning judo.

Don't panic! It's not as difficult as it sounds.

You'll be using Japanese words as you speak to your sensei (coach) and other judoka (judo players) before you know it.

This book will teach you the Japanese names for parts of the body too. Plus there are lots of commands to learn.

You will need to know these words to get your next belt. So, without further ado - let's begin.

Or in Japanese, you would say: "Hajime!"

-BY-

NIK FAIRBROTHER MBE
WORLD CHAMPION 1993
OLYMPIC SILVER MEDALLIST 1992
TRIPLE EUROPEAN CHAMPION

柔道

THE GENTLE WAY

Judo means the Gentle Way. Ju means softness and do means way. Here are some more words to get you going:

Judo	The Gentle Way
Kodokan	Place of Study
Gokyo No Waza	Judo Syllabus
Kata	Movement form
Kanji	Japanese writing
Sushi	Japanese dish

YOUR JUDOGI

You wear a judogi when you go to judo. Wear your zori until the edge of the mat and don't forget to tie your obi.

Judogi	Judo Suit
Obi	Belt
Eri	Collar
Sode	Sleeve
Zori	Footwear

more books at

THE DOJO

When you first enter the **dojo**, you will see your **sensei** and lots of other **judoka** on the **tatami**.

Dojo	Judo Hall
Judoka	Judo Player
Sensei	Judo Coach
Tatami	Judo Mat
Jigoro Kano	Founder of judo

more books at

www.kokakids.co.uk

FIRST CLASS

Listen to your sensei, who will tell you when to hajime and when to matte and will teach you ukemi.

Rei	Bow
Hajime	Begin
Matte	Stop/Break
Sore Made	The End
Sona Mama	Freeze
Yoshi	Un Freeze
Ukemi	Breakfalls

more books at

www.kokakids.co.uk

TORI & UKE

During a judo class you can be both tori and uke. Make sure you learn techniques both migi and hidari.

Tori	Attacker
Uke	Receiver
Migi	Right
Hidari	Left

UKE

TORI

more books at

NE-WAZA

Ne-waza techniques include turnovers and Osaekomi
(eg. Kesa Gatame and Kuzure Kesa Gatame.)

Ne-waza	Groundwork
Osaekomi	Hold Downs
Toketa	Hold Broken
Kuzure	Modified Hold
Fusegi	Escape

more books at

www.kokakids.co.uk

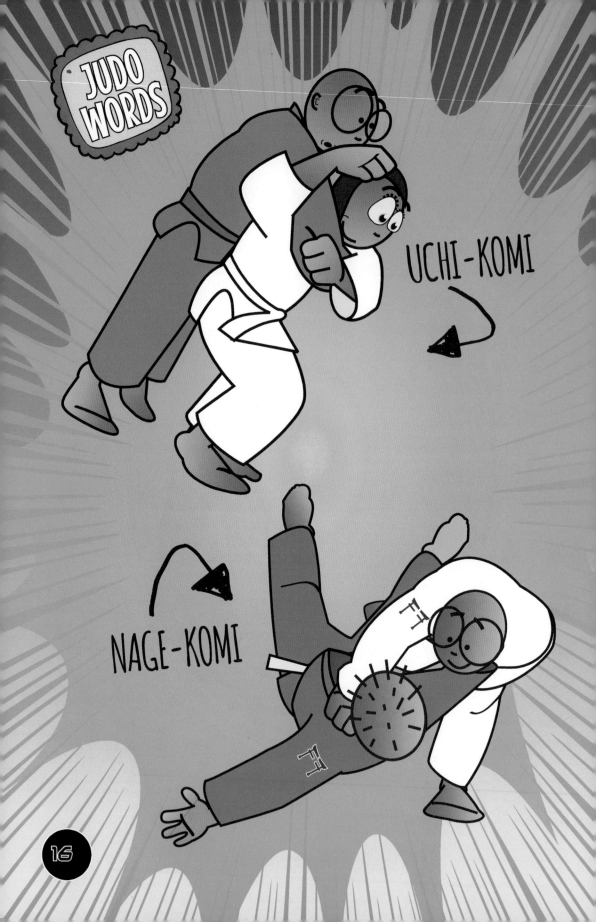

TACHI-WAZA

Tachi-waza means standing judo. Practise your waza by doing lots of uchi-komi and nage-komi.

Waza	Technique
Tachi-waza	Standing Techniques
Nage-Komi	Throwing
Uchi-Komi	Repetition
Tokui Waza	Favourite Waza

STAGES

Every waza has stages. First focus on kuzushi, then perfect the tsukuri and finally the kake.

Kuzushi	Unbalancing
Tsukuri	Entry
Kake	Execution
Tsugi Ashi	Stepping Pattern
Kumi-Kata	Gripping
Jigotai	Defensive posture
Tai-Sabaki	Hip Block

more books at

WAZA

Throws can be classified into these five groups. How many ashi-waza can you do? Do you know any kaeshi-waza?

Te-Waza	Hand Techniques
Koshi-Waza	Hip Techniques
Ashi-Waza	Foot Techniques
Sutemi-Waza	Sacrifice Throws
Kaeshi-Waza	Counter Throws

more books at

www.kokakids.co.uk

TRAINING

Improve your technique by using these training methods. Remember **randori** is not a contest – experiment to learn!

Randori	Free Practise
Tandoku Renshu	Shadow Judo
Renraku-Waza	Combination (same direction)
Renzoku-Waza	Combination (different direction)
Geiko	Free Style

more books at

www.kokakids.co.uk

SHIAI

Aim to score an **ippon** in your next **shiai**. Make sure you don't get a **shido!**

Shiai	Contest
Ippon	Full Point
Waza-Ari	Half Point
Yuko	Score
Shido	Penalty
Hansoku-Make	Disqualification
Hiki-Wake	Draw
Hantei	Call for Decision

more books at

BODY PARTS

By learning how to tell your **hiza** from your **mune** you will understand techniques like **Hiza**-Guruma or **Mune**-Gatame

Ashi	Foot
Hiza	Knee
Kata	Shoulder
Mune	Chest
Koshi	Hip
Ude	Arm
Waki	Armpit

more books at

www.kokakids.co.uk

GRADING

Junior judoka are ranked by Mon Grades, Aim to, one day get your Dan Grade. The highest grade is Judan.

Mon	Junior Grade
Kyu	Student Grade
Dan	Black Belt Grade
Shodan	1st Dan
Rokudan	6th Dan
Hachidan	8th Dan
Kudan	9th Dan
Judan	10th Dan

more books at

SPIRIT

Scream a Kiai at the top of your voice to gather your Fudoshin but never forget to show proper Reiho.

Jita Kyoei	Mutual prosperity
Kiai	Shout to show spirit
Fudoshin	Immovable spirit
Bushido	Way of the Warrior
Seiryoku Zenyo	Maximum efficiency
Joseki	Place of honour
Reiho	Forms of Etiquette
Seika Tanden	Centre of gravity

more books at

PLEASE!

If you have liked this book, please leave a review on Amazon, this helps promote judo and the books.

THANK YOU!

BY

NIK FAIRBROTHER MBE
WORLD CHAMPION 1993
OLYMPIC SILVER MEDALLIST 1992
TRIPLE EUROPEAN CHAMPION

MORE iN THE SERiES!

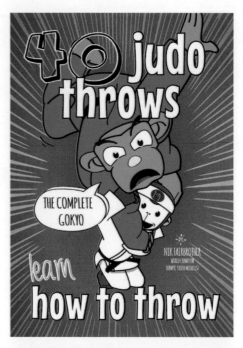

MORE iN THE SERiES!

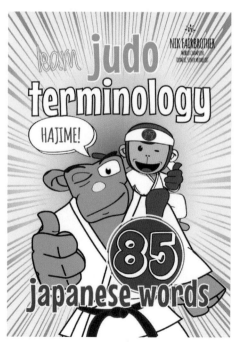

instagram: **kokakidsjudobooks**

facebook: **Koka Kids Junior Judo**

website: **www.kokakids.co.uk**